BRINCANDO
COM INGLÊS

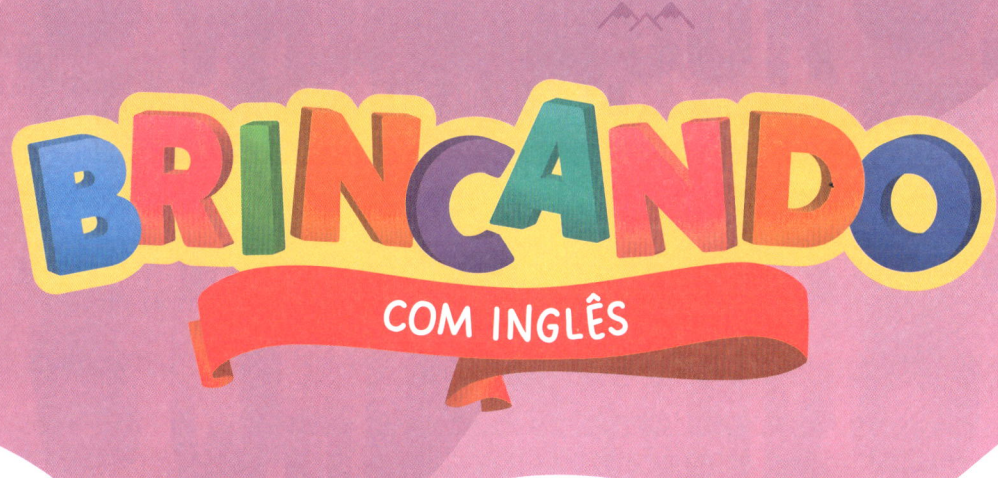

WORKBOOK

3

EDUCAÇÃO INFANTIL

RENATO MENDES CURTO JÚNIOR
ANNA CAROLINA GUIMARÃES
CIBELE MENDES

Editora do Brasil

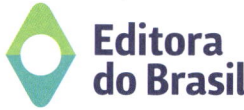

CONTENTS

UNIT 1
SCHOOL FRIENDS **3**

UNIT 2
FUN TIME **7**

UNIT 3
ONLINE GAMES **10**

UNIT 4
MY HEROES **14**

UNIT 5
FAMILY VACATION **18**

UNIT 6
HEALTHY FOOD **22**

UNIT 7
A VISIT TO THE
AQUARIUM **25**

UNIT 8
TRASH? OH NO! **29**

UNIT 1 SCHOOL FRIENDS

1 MAKE A MINIATURE OF THE SCHOOL BUS!

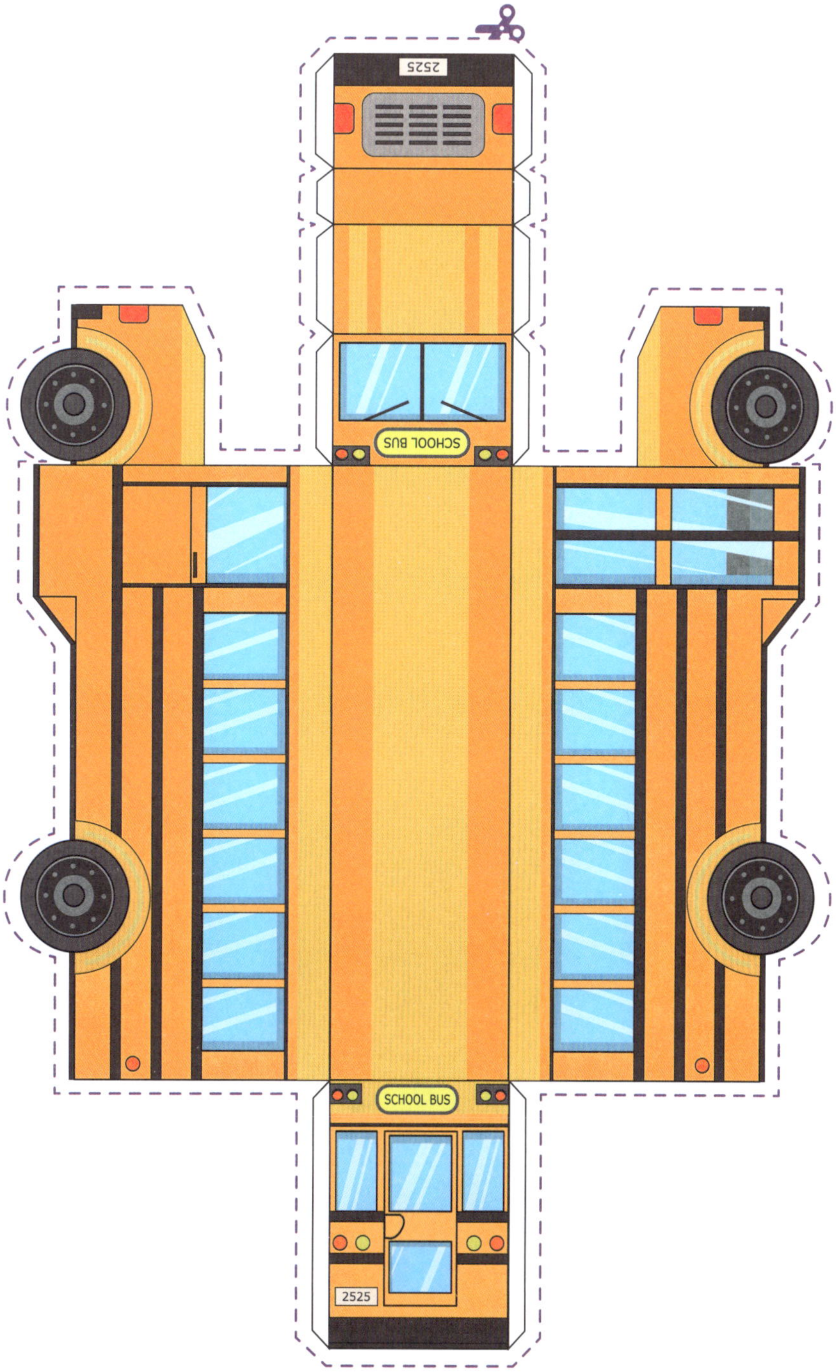

Betsart/Shutterstock.com

2 WRITE THE FEELINGS.

HAPPY

SMART

SAD

BRAVE

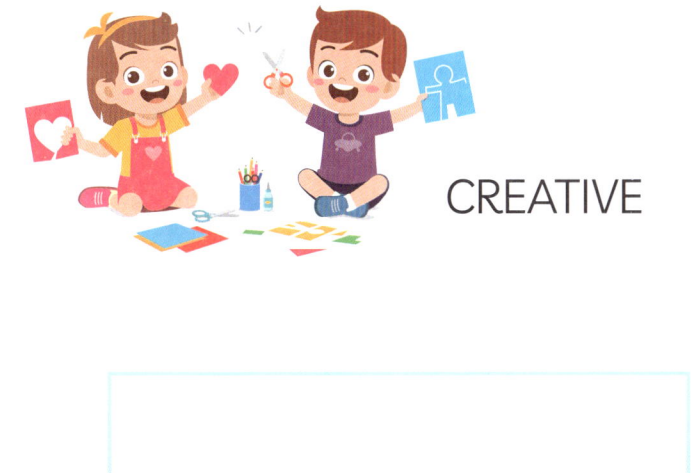

CREATIVE

FEARFUL

FIVE

3 MATCH THE CLOTHES WITH THE SCHOOL OBJECTS OF THE SAME COLOR.

A BLUE RULER

AN ORANGE BOOK

A GREEN PEN

A RED PENCIL CASE

A PINK BACKPACK

FUN TIME

UNIT 2

1 TRACE THE WORDS AND COLOR THE CORRESPONDING IMAGES.

 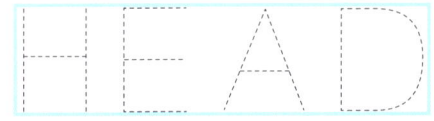

 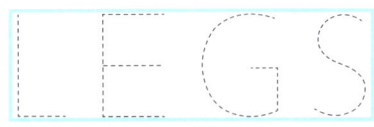

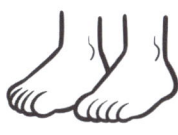 

 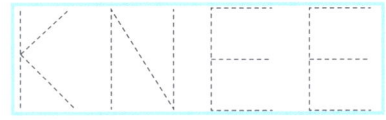

SEVEN 7

❷ COLOR THE SPOTS. THEN TRACE THE WORD.

Ideario Lab

THIS IS A BIKE

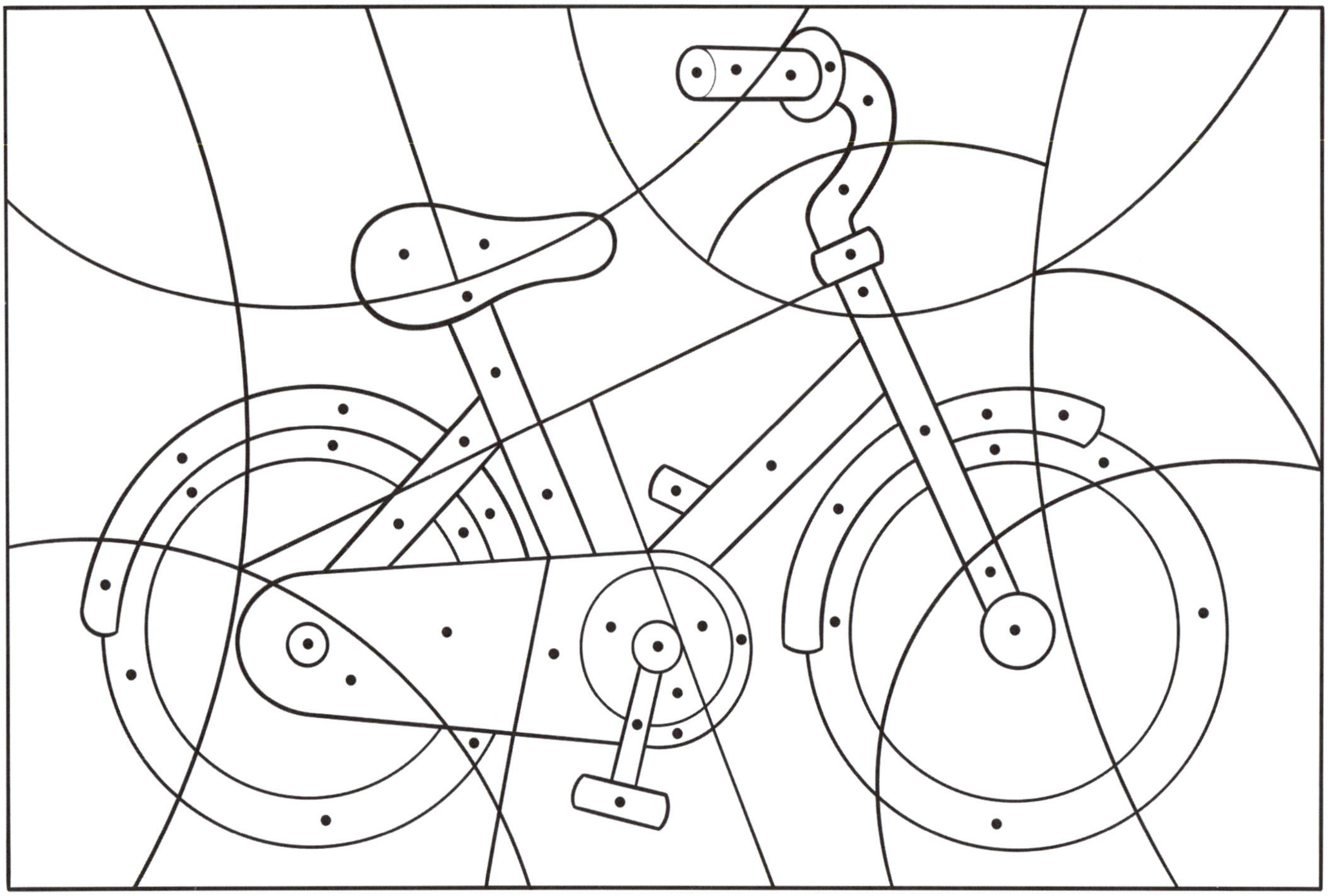

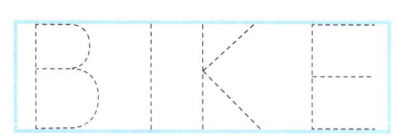

3 CLAP. WHICH PART OF THE BODY DO YOU USE? TRACE.

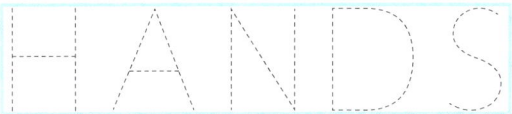

DRAW YOUR HANDS.

UNIT 3

ONLINE GAMES

1 WHAT OBJECT IS THIS? COLOR THE OBJECTS AND MATCH.

Ideario Lab

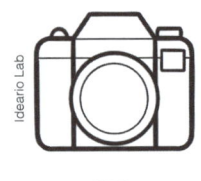

EARPHONES

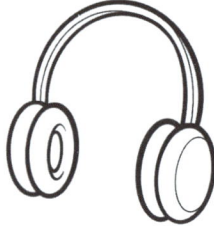

REMOTE CONTROL

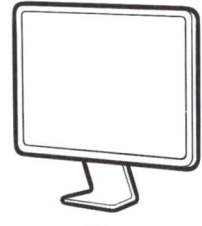

USB

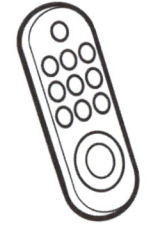

CAMERA

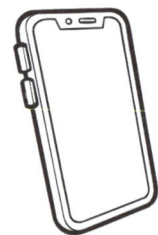

COMPUTER SCREEN

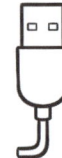

MOBILE PHONE

2 WHERE DO WE SEE THESE IMAGES?

Studio_G/Shutterstock.com

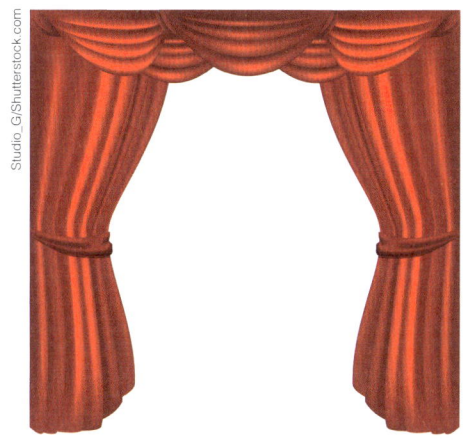

- [ ] THEATER.
- [ ] CLASSROOM.

magicinfoto/Shutterstock.com

- [ ] GYMNASIUM.
- [ ] CLASSROOM.

Iconic Bestiary/Shutterstock.com

- [ ] THEATER.
- [ ] HOME.

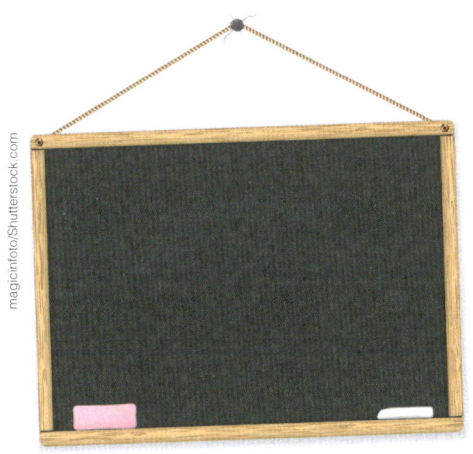

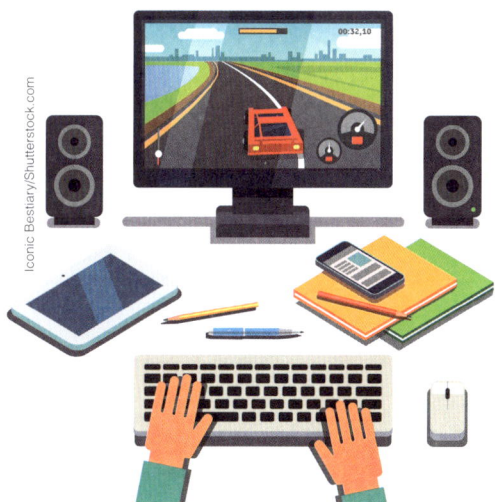

3 HOW MANY ARE THERE IN THE IMAGE?

 **STARS**

THERE ARE _____ STARS.

 **HEARTS**

THERE ARE _____ HEARTS.

 **CLOUDS**

THERE ARE _____ CLOUDS.

 **TREES**

THERE ARE _____ TREES.

4 COMPLETE THE MISSING NUMBERS.

5 HOW MANY ARE THERE? COUNT AND WRITE THE NUMBERS.

THIRTEEN 13

UNIT 4

MY HEROES

1 COLOR THE IMAGE ACCORDING TO THE EXAMPLE.

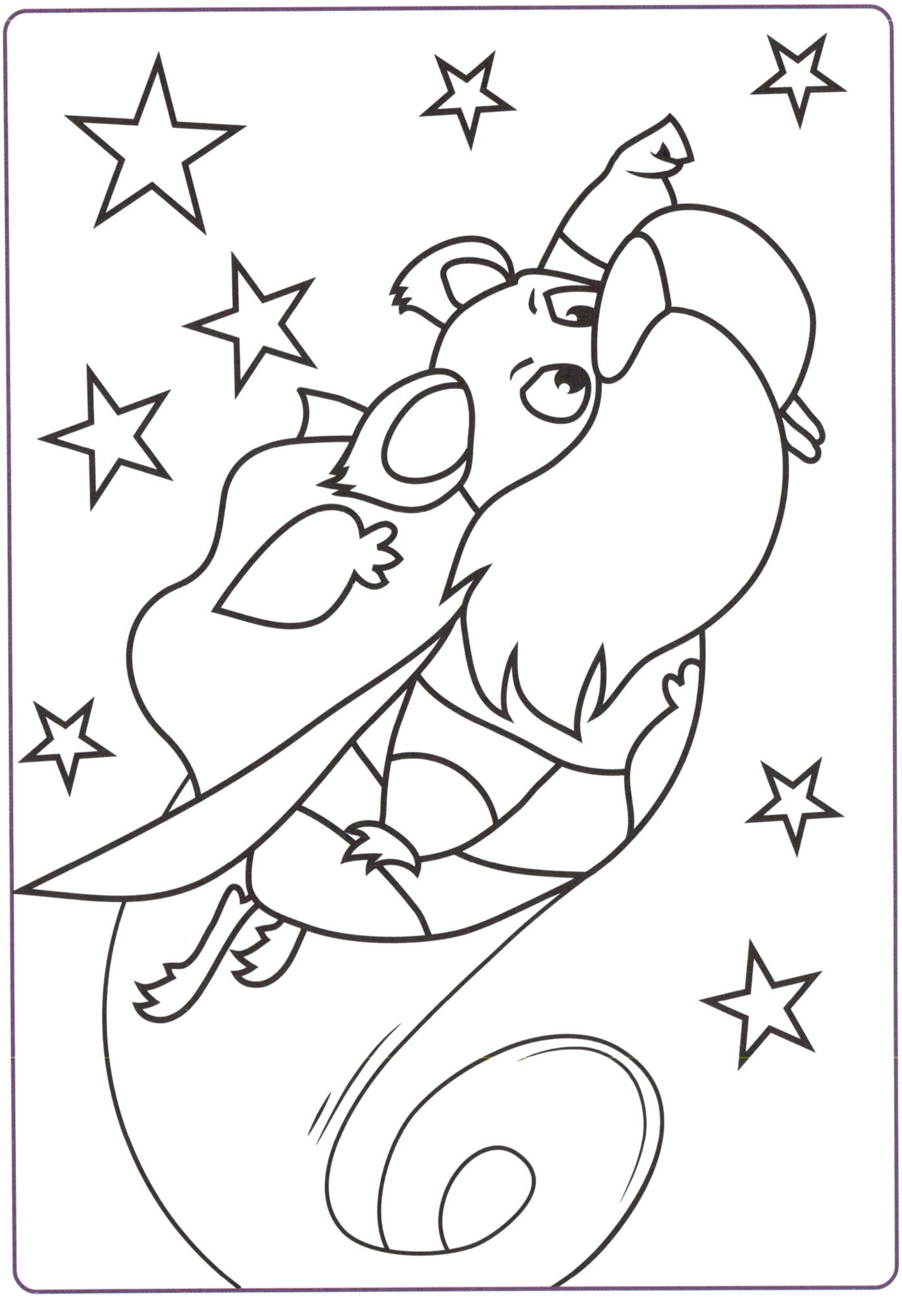

Leh/Shutterstock.com

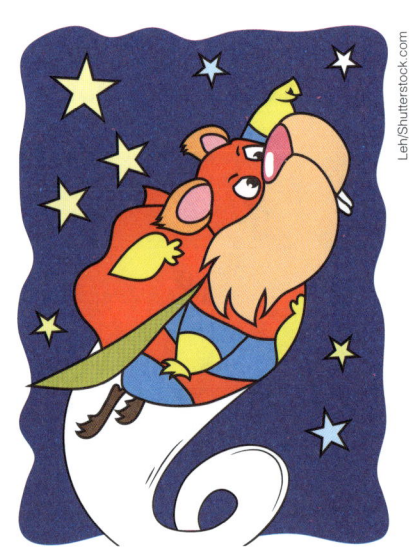

2 TRACE THE NAMES.

cloverlittleworld/Shutterstock.com

PRINCESS

PRINCE

FoxyImage/Shutterstock.com

HERO

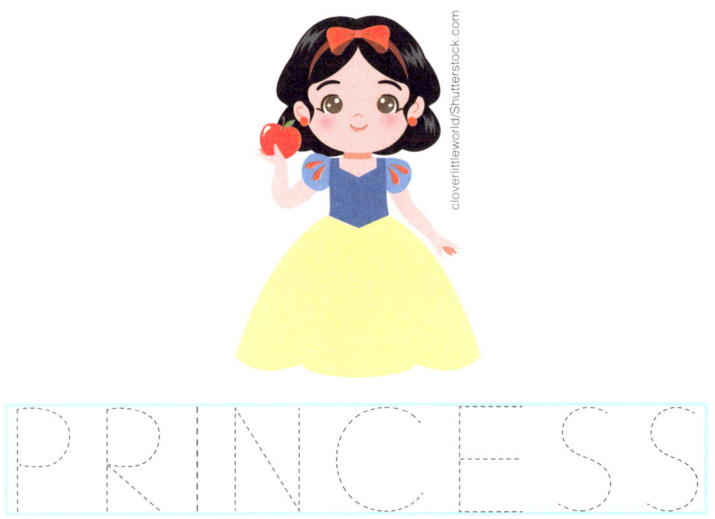

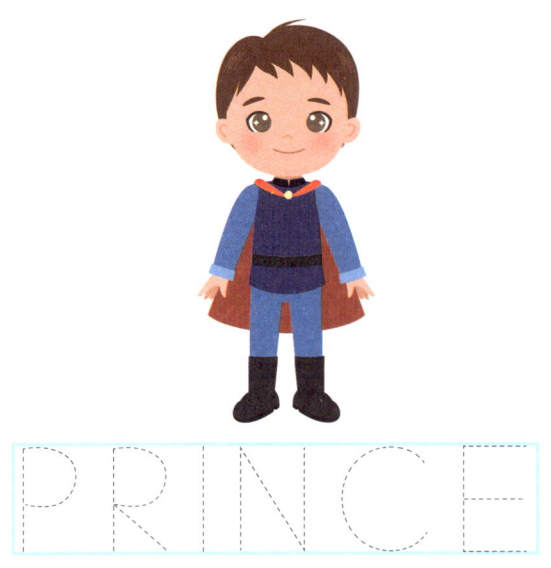

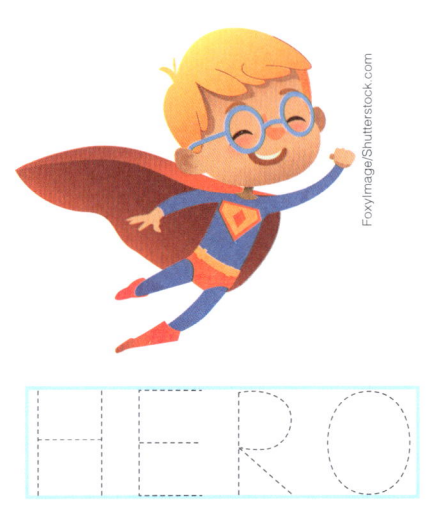

3 COMPLETE THE NAMES WITH **H** OR **P**.

___EART

___EN

___AT

___IG

___ICTURE

___ORSE

4 CIRCLE AND PAINT ACCORDING TO THE NUMBER.

8

Lesya Mashtakova/Shutterstock.com

10

MMolivasiA/Shutterstock.com

2

Domira/Shutterstock.com

5

Lexi Claus/Shutterstock.com

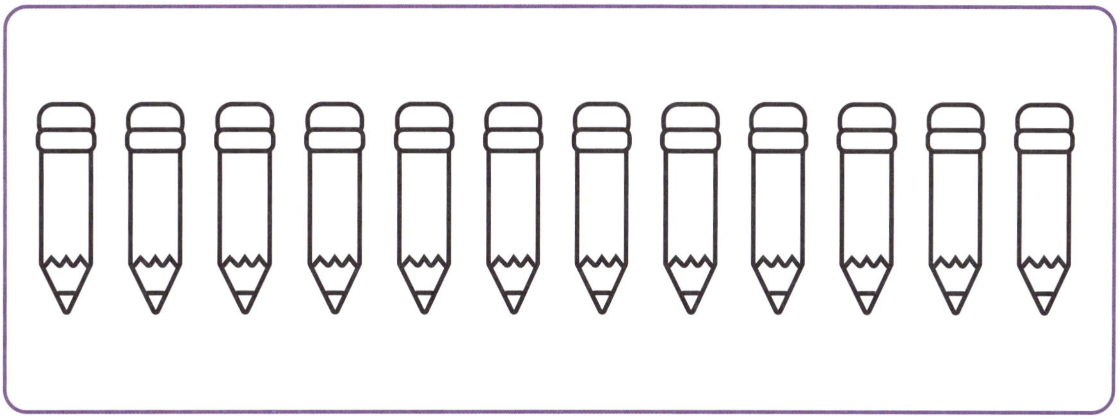

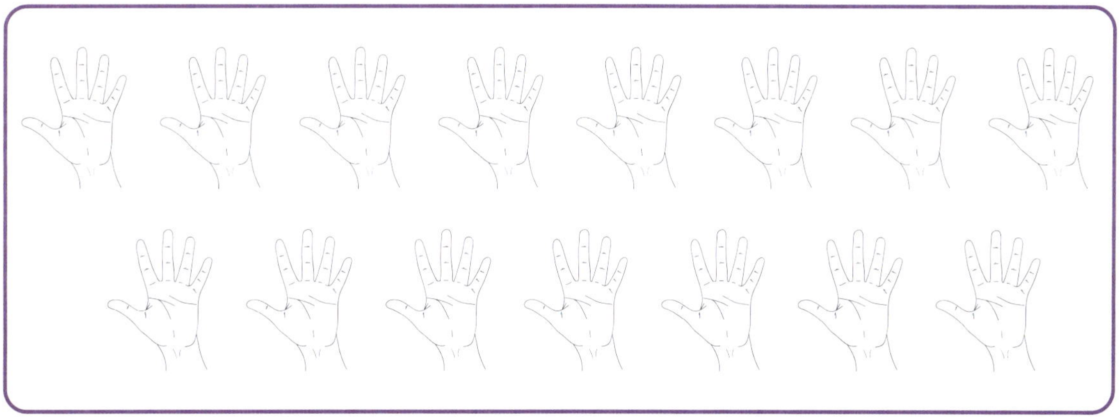

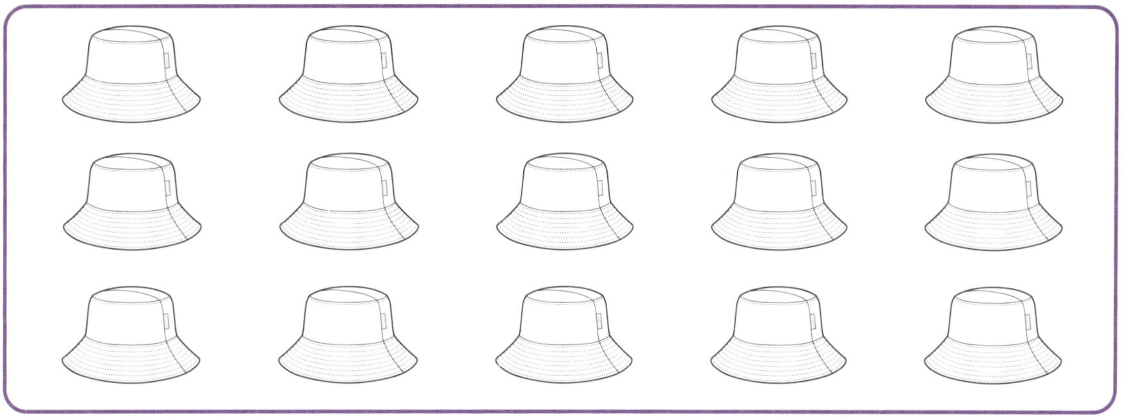

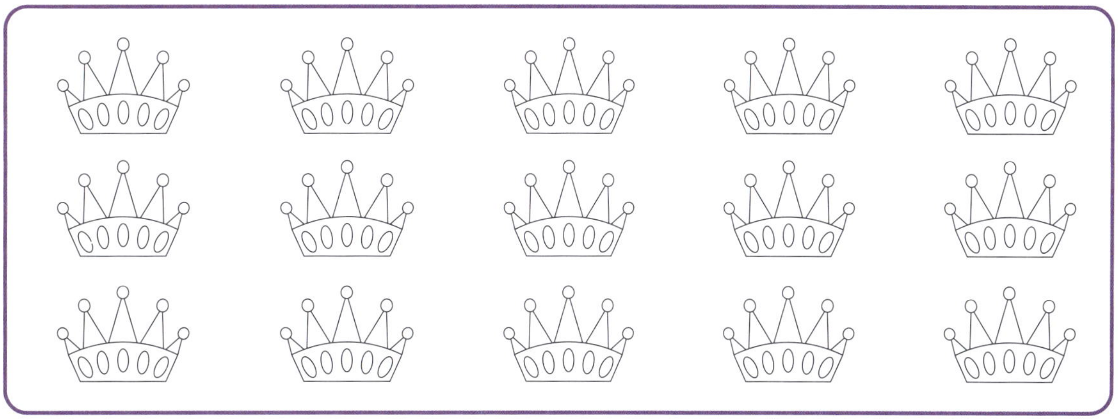

UNIT 5 FAMILY VACATION

1 MATCH THE IMAGES WITH THEIR NAMES. AFTER THAT, COLOR THEM.

AIRPLANE

CAR

BUS

TRAIN

18 EIGHTEEN

2 FAMILY TRIP! COLOR THE SUITCASE, THEN SEARCH IN NEWSPAPERS OR MAGAZINES FOR OBJECTS YOU WOULD LIKE TO TAKE. CUT THEM OUT AND PASTE THEM ON THE SUITCASE.

3 WHERE ARE YOU GOING? COMPLETE THE ANSWER.

NINETEEN 19

4 TRACE THE WORDS AND COLOR THE IMAGE ACCORDING TO THE LABELS.

THE CAR IS RED.

THE TREES ARE GREEN.

THE SKY IS BLUE.

THE SUN IS YELLOW.

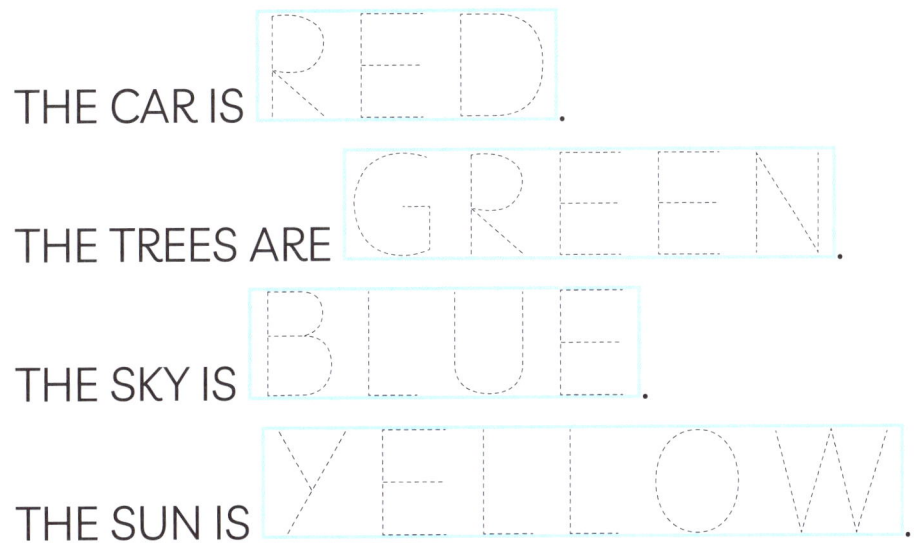

TWENTY-ONE 21

UNIT 6 HEALTHY FOOD

1 READ THE NAMES OF THE FRUITS AND DRAW THEM.

APPLE	PEAR
PAPAYA	BANANA
MANGO	WATERMELON

2. COUNT AND MARK.

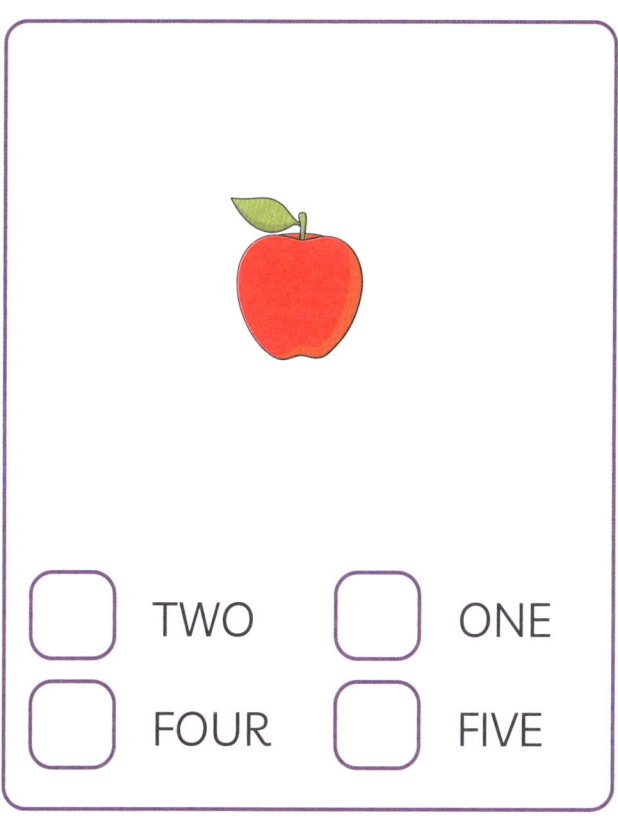

- ☐ TWO
- ☐ ONE
- ☐ FOUR
- ☐ FIVE

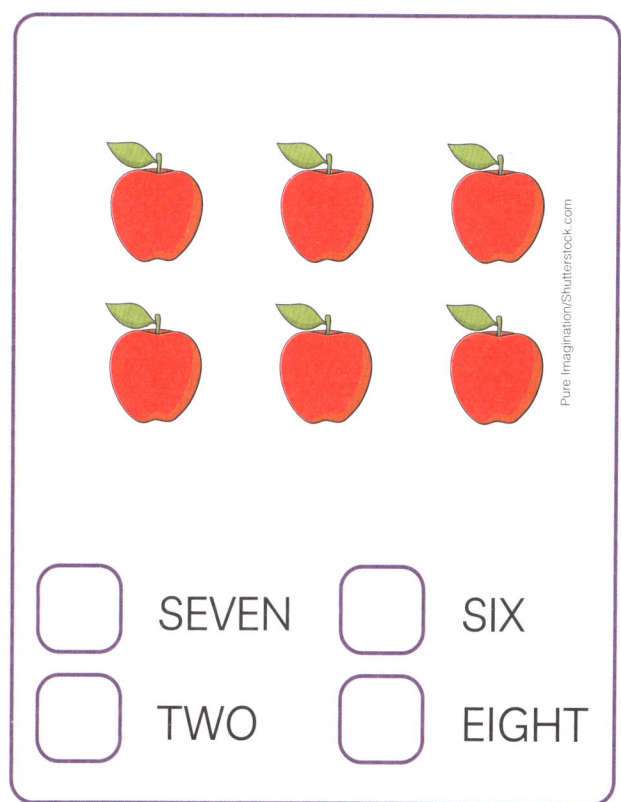

- ☐ SEVEN
- ☐ SIX
- ☐ TWO
- ☐ EIGHT

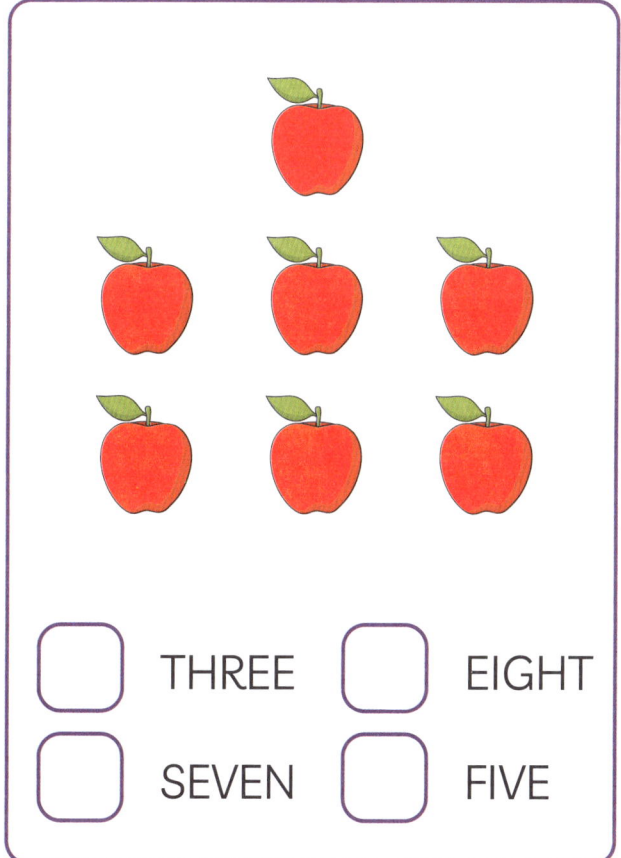

- ☐ THREE
- ☐ EIGHT
- ☐ SEVEN
- ☐ FIVE

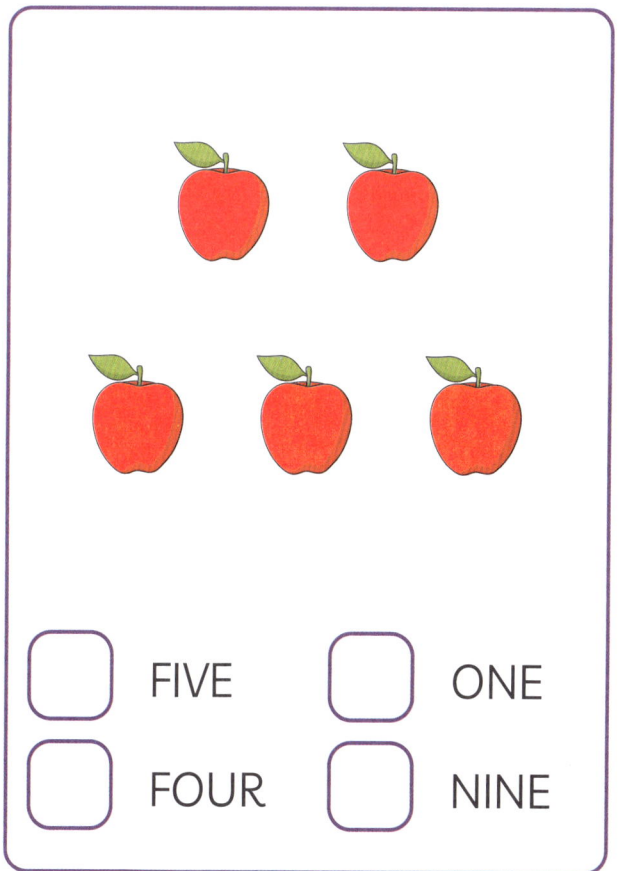

- ☐ FIVE
- ☐ ONE
- ☐ FOUR
- ☐ NINE

3 MATCH.

   APPLE

   ORANGE

   GRAPE

   BANANA

   WATERMELON

   MANGO

A VISIT TO THE AQUARIUM

UNIT 7

1 WHO ARE THESE SEA ANIMALS? CHECK.

☐ SHARK
☐ SEA TURTLE

☐ FISH
☐ SEAHORSE

☐ SEAHORSE
☐ SEA TURTLE

☐ SHARK
☐ FISH

TWENTY-FIVE 25

2 DRAW YOUR FAVORITE FISH, THEN COLOR THE SCENE.

WHAT IS THE NAME OF YOUR FAVORITE FISH?

3 MAKE A PUZZLE ACCORDING TO THE IMAGE BELOW. THEN, SOLVE IT!

TWENTY-SEVEN 27

TRASH? OH NO!

UNIT 8

1 SORT OUT THE WASTE.

Photoroyalty/Shutterstock.com

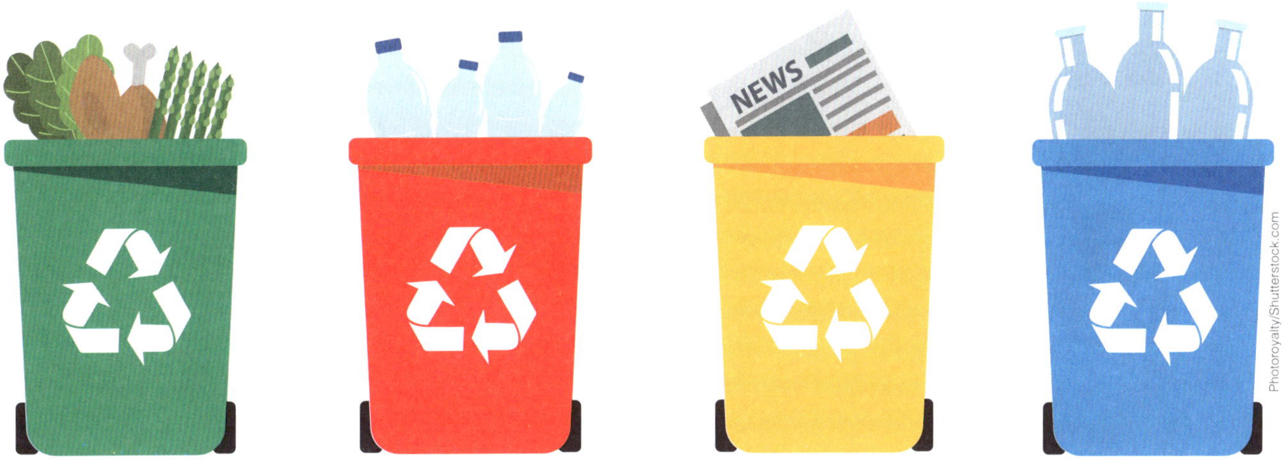

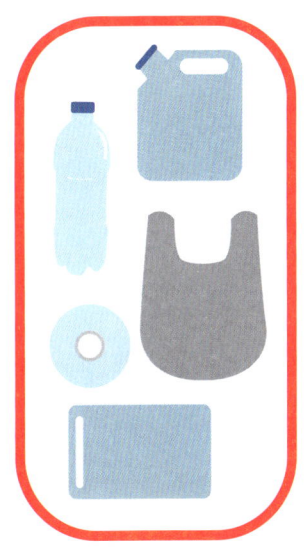

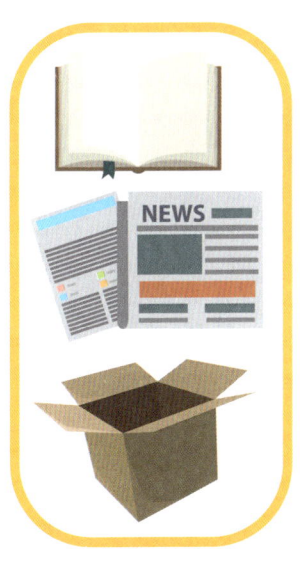

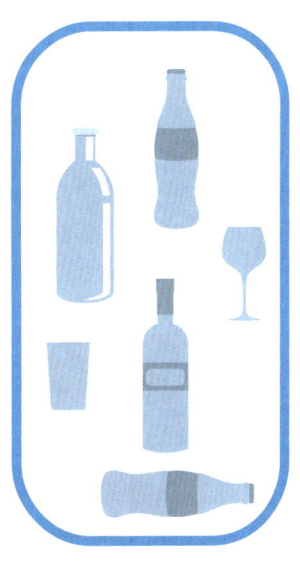

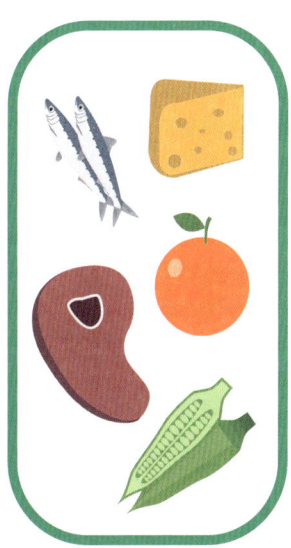

2. WHAT MATERIAL IS IT?

☐ PLASTIC   ☐ GLASS
☐ PAPER   ☐ METAL

☐ PLASTIC   ☐ METAL
☐ PAPER   ☐ ORGANIC

☐ PLASTIC   ☐ GLASS
☐ ORGANIC   ☐ METAL

☐ PLASTIC   ☐ GLASS
☐ PAPER   ☐ METAL

☐ PLASTIC   ☐ GLASS
☐ PAPER   ☐ ORGANIC

3 YOU NEED TO THROW AWAY A PIECE OF GARBAGE.

1. WRITE DOWN THE NAME OF THE GARBAGE.
2. COLOR THE RECICLYING BIN ACCORDING TO THE WASTE TO BE DISPOSED OF.
3. CUT OUT PICTURES OF THE WASTE TO BE DISPOSED OF AND PASTE THEM IN THE RECYCLING BIN.

THIRTY-ONE 31